Old Sarum

WILTSHIRE

DEREK RENN CBE, PhD, FSA

High above Salisbury Plain stands Old Sarum, the site of the ancient city of Salisbury. In the Iron Age a massive hillfort was created here, which was later occupied by Romans and Saxons, before being chosen by the Normans for the site of a motte-and-bailey castle. Old Sarum was to grow into one of the most flourishing settlements in early medieval England, as castle, cathedral, and thriving township. Later it was eclipsed by the new city of Salisbury, and by the nineteenth century had become one of the most notorious 'rotten boroughs' in the land.

This handbook describes and illustrates all the buildings which once stood here: those of the castle inner bailey in the middle, the cathedral next to it and the outer earthworks and gates. It tells the story of how and why Old Sarum was altered at different times, why it was abandoned and how it was unearthed again; and it describes some of the people who lived here. Finally, something is said about plans for its future. There is a list of further reading at the end of the book for those who wish to follow up any part of the story.

ENGLISH HERITAGE · LONDON

Contents

**A brief tour of Old Sarum
is given on pages 18–19
(centre pages)**

Published by English Heritage,
23 Savile Row, London W1X 1AB
Copyright © English Heritage 1994
First published by English Heritage 1994, reprinted 1995, reprinted 1999

Photographs by English Heritage Photography Section
and copyright of English Heritage unless otherwise stated

Printed in England by The White Dove Press
KJ C140   7/99   FA5703
ISBN 1 85074 460 2

Introduction

Visiting Old Sarum (Old Salisbury) is an evocative experience: people have lived on this windswept hilltop off and on for 5000 years. The enormous banks and ditches which surround the site were created, through tremendous co-operative efforts, by prehistoric people who needed to protect themselves and their cattle. The Romans had a settlement of some kind here, and several Roman roads converge on the site. In Saxon times a town grew up within the prehistoric ramparts. It was strengthened against the Vikings and escaped attack by the Danish king Sweyn, who sacked neighbouring towns in 1003.

Soon after the Conquest, the Normans began to build a royal castle at Old Sarum. William the Conqueror paid off his troops here, and some years later he summoned all landholders to give him their oath of loyalty. Two palaces and a cathedral were built, and Old Sarum

Essential dates	
	(BC)
Neolithic settlement	about 3000
Iron Age hillfort (outer banks)	about 500
	(AD)
Norman castle begun (inner mound)	by 1070
Cathedral begun	1075
Move to Salisbury	1219
Castle demolished	1514
Rotten borough abolished	1832
Placed in State care	1892

became a thriving medieval city. Although the bishop moved his cathedral to the town of (New) Salisbury in 1219, a few people continued to live at Old Sarum and to send members to Parliament until 1832.

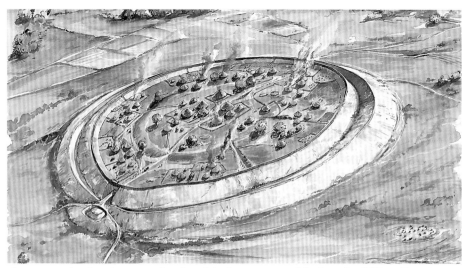

A reconstruction drawing suggesting the original appearance of the Iron Age hillfort (Peter Dunn)

What to See

There are three main areas to see at Old Sarum: the prehistoric outer earthworks; the inner bailey of the Norman castle (on the mound at the centre of the site); and the cathedral, beyond the inner bailey to the north-west. You are free to explore these in any order, staying within the fenced area or along the waymarked footpaths outside. (For your own safety, however, please do not climb on the walls, or go near the edges of pits or ditches.)

This section of the handbook describes all the main features of the site (numbered in brackets). For quick reference the bird's-eye view on the centre pages shows you where everything is, using the same numbers. The buildings are described in the order you are most likely to come to them, starting with the inner bailey of the Norman castle.

Castle dates

First castle (timber)	1069/70
Keep built	1100
Royal Palace built in stone	1130–39
Major repairs	1170–1208
Castleguard lapses	1255
Gaol closed	1450
Final demolition	1514

The Norman castle

After you left the main road, you came into Old Sarum as people have done for over 2000 years, through the entrance gap in the prehistoric hillfort defences (the East Gate) **(1)**. The Normans took advantage of these existing defences when,

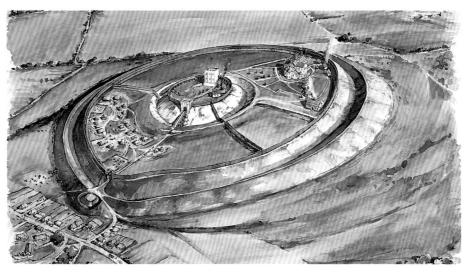

Old Sarum as it might have appeared about 1100. The inner bailey and earliest castle buildings have been constructed within the Iron Age ramparts, and the first cathedral has been completed (Peter Dunn)

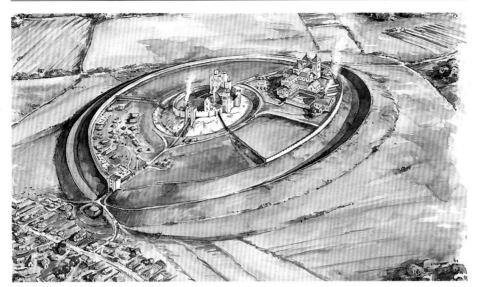

Old Sarum as it might have appeared about 1130. The Royal Palace (in the inner bailey) and a larger cathedral have been built. The town outside the city walls is growing (Peter Dunn)

in the eleventh century, they chose the site for their new castle. The huge earth banks were adapted to become the outer perimeter walls of the castle and town, and an inner stronghold was created on a mound in the centre. The area on the mound formed an inner bailey (or courtyard) while part of the area outside, including the area now occupied by the car park (2), was used as an outer bailey.

Many Norman castles consisted of a mound topped by a single tower, and an outer bailey containing the domestic buildings. At Old Sarum the mound was made large enough to contain several sizeable buildings. It was created by digging a deep ditch and throwing the spoil upwards and inwards, and was further strengthened by a timber wall on top, backed with earth.

The number of people living in the castle varied enormously. In 1070, when William the Conqueror paid off his troops here, a whole army camped in the outer bailey. On other occasions the king and his retinue or the county sheriff might stay for a limited period. More often the household of the castle would consist only of a small standing garrison under the control of the constable. Because of this variation in numbers, the accommodation (and supplies) offered by the castle had to be flexible.

The gatehouse

The gatehouse (3) can best be appreciated from the outside, standing on the bridge which leads up to the inner bailey. This was the main entrance to the castle, a strong and imposing building which towered high above the heads of any attackers. A turret, rising above the level of the roof, was attached to the inner left-hand corner. The gatehouse was approached by a wooden drawbridge which worked on a pivot (like a see-saw); when the bridge was raised up in times of danger it would have blocked the entrance-way and left a gap too wide to

The castle gatehouse as it might have appeared about 1130 (Peter Dunn)

cross. You can still see the stone base that supported the drawbridge, underneath the modern bridge.

The gatehouse was designed around a central passage, with doors at either end. Both sets of doors opened inwards for security and were barred with long timber beams which slid out from holes in the side walls. Leading off from the passage to the sides were guard-chambers with vaulted (arched) ceilings. There was at least one upper floor, containing well-proportioned, comfortable rooms; these may have been used by the constable, who was responsible for the castle's security.

The inner bailey

Having passed through the gatehouse, you enter the central courtyard of the inner bailey (4). In the early Middle Ages this was a place of bustling activity. Around the edges you can see the remains of several buildings. Opposite you is the Great Tower or keep, while to your right, on two levels, is the Royal Palace. Around

the perimeter is a stone wall, part of the inner bailey's defence system.

The first castle buildings were all made of timber, but most were later rebuilt in stone. The earliest stone buildings were the gatehouse and keep. The Royal Palace was completely rebuilt in stone in the early twelfth century, as were the wooden defences around the perimeter, in the late twelfth century. The upper parts of all these grand buildings have been demolished but the lower parts remain, although their original appearance would have been very different. What you see today is the flint core of the walls; these were originally faced with good-quality stone and probably whitewashed. The exterior surfaces would therefore have appeared much whiter and smoother than now. This outer stone was rare and expensive, and once the castle was abandoned it was carried off to be used elsewhere.

Just to the left of the Royal Palace is the main castle well. It may have been over 200ft (60m) deep. It has only been partly excavated, and the water you see now is simply drainage from the inner bailey and not the true level of water percolating through the chalk. Water supply was a great problem at Old Sarum because of the depth of the water table below the top of the hill. Rainwater from the castle roofs was probably channelled into tubs and barrels.

The Royal Palace

The first building on the site of the Royal Palace (5) dated from the early days of the castle. Known as the 'king's house', it was probably constructed of timber on stone foundations. By 1070 it was already well enough furnished for William the Conqueror to be in residence: documents tell us that in that year he sealed a legal deed here.

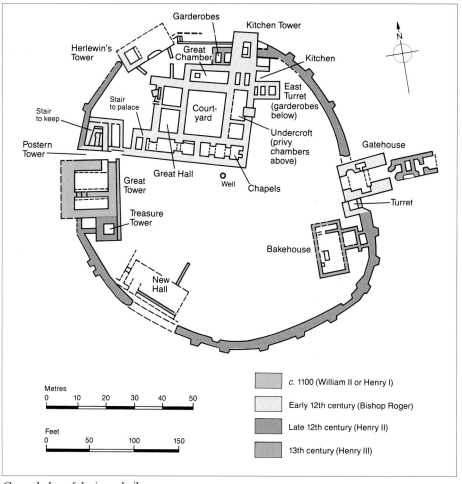

Ground plan of the inner bailey

About sixty years later the palace was rebuilt on a grander scale by the king's chancellor, Bishop Roger. Roger was the powerful and influential third bishop of Old Sarum, who held office from 1107–39 (see p 28). As bishop and chancellor, he had authority not only over the church but in many secular matters too, and he effectively controlled the castle as well as the cathedral. Roger's rebuilding of the Royal Palace was an ambitious project; he probably intended it to provide luxurious accommodation for King Henry I, whose patronage had placed him in his present favoured position. More usually, when the king was not in residence, the palace buildings would have served as the offices and lodgings of the county sheriff (the king's agent). Some of the rooms would have been used for more than one purpose; a hall by day might become a dormitory by night.

Understanding the foundations is complicated by the fact that they are on two levels. The palace consisted of four ranges built around a central square courtyard. This courtyard, and the north and west ranges, were on the upper level, while the south and east ranges were on the lower level. The buildings on the upper level had only one storey, while the buildings on the lower level had two, so that the roof was more or less level. The four ranges of buildings were linked by covered corridors, like a cathedral cloister.

The outside of the palace was faced with carefully squared stones which were then whitewashed for protection. The inner walls were sometimes just made of flint nodules mortared together, but plastered over and painted to look like smooth stone. The roofs were covered with stone slabs, shale slates and clay tiles, those along the roof ridges being glazed red or green. We have no evidence of how the rooms were decorated and furnished, but they would probably have had painted scenes on the walls and textile hangings for warmth.

The arrangement of the rooms inside the palace reflects the formality of life in the royal household. Those of lesser status

The Royal Palace today. The south and east ranges are in the foreground, with the well in front

would have been allowed to enter only the public rooms, while those with higher connections would have had access to rooms of greater privacy, where relations with the king were less distant and formal. Only the king's closest associates, his immediate family and his personal servants would have entered his privy chambers. This sequence of rooms – from the most formal to the most intimate – provided an elaborate stage on which the king's complex social relationships could be acted out.

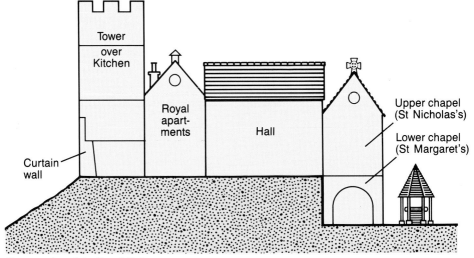

Cross-section of the Royal Palace

The castle courtyard as it might have appeared about 1130. The Royal Palace is on the right and the keep straight ahead. Note the Postern Tower on the right of the keep (Peter Dunn)

At the far end of the two-storey south range was a forebuilding containing a staircase. This led to the upper rooms of the palace (you can now climb up on to the bank at this point). It also linked the palace to the Postern Tower and keep (see p 10), via a porch and gallery. This is where medieval visitors would have entered the palace. The first room they would have come to was the Great Hall, a large public room where formal meals would have been held and official business conducted. From the Great Hall, more privileged visitors would have progressed to the Great Chamber in the north range. Here the king would have received them in more intimate surroundings (although still with much formality and ritual). The chamber may have contained a state bed, perhaps behind a screen.

Beyond the Great Chamber was the two-storey east range, containing the private royal apartments. Here, on the upper courtyard level, the king and his family would have slept and dined privately, away from the affairs of state. Beneath the apartments (and now visible on the lower level) was the palace kitchen, which contained several large fireplaces. These would have warmed the royal apartments all year round.

To the north of the east range, against the perimeter wall, was a high tower known as the 'tower over the kitchen'. On either side of the tower is a set of

One of two pairs of sewage pits in the palace

The remains of the lower chapel

stone-lined pits, originally used for sewage (kept sweet with layers of quicklime). In later years these pits were filled up with medieval rubbish, including broken pottery, glass and ironwork, and also, because of their position near the kitchen, fish, animal and bird bones – the remnants of many a feast.

At the southern end of the east range were two chapels, one above the other. St Nicholas's Chapel (on the upper courtyard level) was for the use of the royal household, and could be reached directly from the private apartments. In this chapel, records tell us, a light constantly burned. Underneath on the ground level was a second chapel, St Margaret's, which would have been used for public worship. It could be reached from the main castle courtyard and had stone benches along the sides and a vaulted roof.

Herlewin's Tower

Only part of the base of this tower survives, up on the bank behind the palace to the north-west. It was originally a large and imposing two-storey building in a prestigious position overlooking the cathedral. It would have provided secure accommodation separate from the palace, and might have been used by the bishop or by an important adult member of the

king's household, such as his mother or eldest son.

The name Herlewin might be either a mispronunciation of Herman (the first bishop of Salisbury), or a reference to Herluin, founder of the famous priory of Bec in Normandy. Herluin died in 1078 just as Osmund (one of his pupils) was made bishop of Salisbury and began to build the cathedral.

The keep or Great Tower

The keep or Great Tower (6) was the first stone building in the inner bailey, and would have provided accommodation for the king before the Royal Palace was built in its present form. The main consideration was security: the keep was located as far as possible from the entrance to the inner bailey and had thick walls which were originally some 50–60ft (15–18m) high. It could be defended from battlements on the roof, and was further

The steep-sided base of the keep

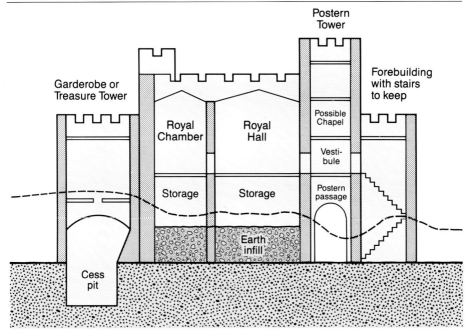

Cross-section of the keep or Great Tower. The dotted line represents the present ground level

protected by the sloping surface of the base of the walls, which would have deflected missiles and made it difficult for attackers to undermine or pick at the wall. In the later part of its life, the keep served as a gaol: a building designed to keep people out was instead used to keep people in.

There is now little to see inside the keep, and one of the outer walls has been demolished completely. However, we do know something about the internal design. The ground floor was completely filled up with earth at an early stage, possibly as soon as the building was completed. Above this were two further floors, containing two rooms each. The first floor was probably used for storage; the upper floor contained the royal apartments.

Postern Tower

Attached to the keep on the right-hand side (as you face it) was a tower known as

the Postern Tower, after the postern passage which ran through the base of it. This was a dark tunnel with gates at either end, which led out to a timber bridge across the castle ditch and gave access to the cathedral and outer West Gate. The passage would have been used occasionally as an alternative entrance to the inner bailey. However, it was very small because of the security risk, and was protected by the tower above. Later, security was tightened by replacing the straight tunnel with a narrow twisting passage which could be more easily guarded.

The entrance to the keep was on the top floor, via the Postern Tower and an adjoining forebuilding. The forebuilding contained a two-flight stone staircase: you can still see the start of the second flight up on the bank to the right. This led into a vestibule in the Postern Tower, and from there straight into the royal

The remains of the staircase leading to the Postern Tower

apartments – probably a Great Hall and a chamber. Although we cannot be certain, the arrangement of other keeps of the same period suggests that there may have been a chapel above the vestibule. The lower floor of the keep was probably accessible only from the second floor.

Garderobe or Treasure Tower

A generation or so after it was built the keep was extended by the addition of

The sewage pit in the Treasure Tower

another tower on the side opposite to the Postern Tower. The new tower contained a private room on each floor, with latrines attached. These 'garderobes' or wardrobe-rooms would have been used for valuable possessions. We know that a treasury was built here, probably on the upper floor, in 1181 or 1182. Its position as far as possible from the main entrance to the keep made it a secure place for valuables. Today only the great arched sewage pit survives.

New Hall and bakery

A long stone wall with a continuous bench is all that is left of the 'New Hall'. This was built in the late twelfth century, and was listed as one of the buildings to be mended in 1247 (when Henry III ordered repairs to be made at Old Sarum). The New Hall was used for public business and also provided temporary extra accommodation.

The rectangular building near the gatehouse was the bakery, placed here to reduce the risk of fire spreading to the other buildings.

Outer bailey and curtain wall

On leaving the inner bailey over the bridge, you come back to the outer bailey of the castle (7). This occupied only a portion of the old Iron Age hillfort, and its boundaries were marked by smaller banks (now covered in trees), radiating from the inner bailey to the outer ramparts. The Iron Age earthworks had already been heightened once before the arrival of the Normans, by the Saxons. The Normans heightened them again, and rebuilt the wooden walls along the top. The outer bailey contained all the service buildings and extra accommodation which could not be fitted into the inner bailey but which were needed to support a lordly estate. It must have been in this area that William the Conqueror's army was paid off in 1070 and where his landholders assembled to give him their oath of loyalty in 1086 (see pages 25 and 27).

An underground passage leads out under the bank from the north-west corner of the outer bailey, but it has been filled in for safety. This passage was on the site of an old entrance into the Iron Age hillfort.

In about 1130 the wooden wall on top of the banks was rebuilt in stone by Bishop Roger. This thick curtain wall (8) extended most of the way round Old Sarum but was not completed, perhaps as a result of Roger's fall from favour in 1139 (see p 28). You can still see one fragment of the wall in the trees behind the site of the cathedral where the Bishop's Palace once stood; it contains big slots which may have supported an overhanging timber gallery.

The cathedral

The cathedral precinct (9) begins beyond the radial bank to the north of the inner bailey.

The first cathedral at Old Sarum was built between 1075 and 1092 by Bishop Osmund (see p 26); it was fairly modest in area but as high as the nearby towers of the castle on their mound. The internal plan consisted of a nave separated from two side aisles by eight great arches on each side. At the east end, the main altar and two side chapels in the cross-arms (or transepts) were enclosed by semi-circular apses.

Only five days after the cathedral was consecrated in 1092, its masonry was shaken by a great storm which destroyed the tower roof. Rebuilding was begun early in the twelfth century by Osmund's successor, Bishop Roger, who doubled the length of the cathedral and made the transepts larger. He built an even higher

The foundations of the cathedral marked out in the grass

*Plans of the first
and second
cathedrals
at Old Sarum*

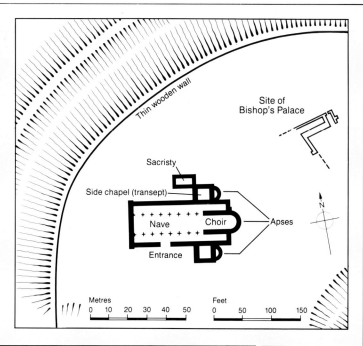

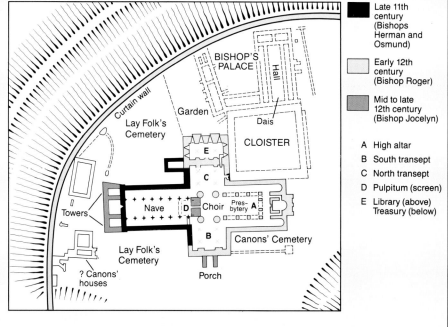

central tower, which now overtopped the castle. The result was a great Norman cathedral, large and grand enough to provide a stage for the elaborate church ceremonies of the time and to hold many people at once. Although it is hard to imagine today, the building that once stood here must have been an inspiring sight. A contemporary writer said that the whole cathedral looked as if it were carved out of a single block, so impressive was the quality of the stonework. The interior was filled with glorious colour.

Only the foundations of the cathedral and cloister, together with the basement of the treasury, survive. The cathedral foundations are marked out in two colours, to distinguish the original building from the later extensions. At the far (western) end you can see the thick walls of the late twelfth-century west front, which had tall flanking towers on either side (these were built by Bishop Jocelyn, Roger's successor). Coming eastwards, the nave of the first cathedral has two rows of cross-shaped bases

The first cathedral as it might have appeared on completion in 1092 (Peter Dunn)

marking the position of the soaring pillars of the aisles. At the end of the rows of bases are the original choir and chapels marked by the semi-circular walls. The four enormous pillar bases here supported the central tower which was added when the cathedral was lengthened and bigger transepts created on either side.

The interior of the second cathedral was magnificently decorated. The walls were clad with red porphyry and green

The second cathedral as it might have appeared in the later twelfth century (Peter Dunn)

Three carved heads from Old Sarum Cathedral (now in Salisbury and South Wilts Museum)

marble, in imitation of contemporary churches in Rome, and the floor was made of alternate slabs of white and green stone, with interlacing circles near the main altar (see illustration on p 27). The altar stood at the east end, raised up on a platform. There was probably a crypt below in which holy relics were kept.

On the north side of the cathedral (away from the castle) is a walled

Wall niche in Bishop Roger's treasury

basement: this is the bottom part of Bishop Roger's treasury, containing its own well. For security the treasury had only tiny windows and was vaulted over to make it fireproof. One of the small wall cupboards survives. The upper floors would have housed the cathedral library and writing-office.

In the angle between the cathedral and the treasury was the cloister (10), also built by Bishop Roger. This was a covered walkway built around an open space; it is now marked out by a trench in the grass. Only one long low piece of wall survives.

The area next to the cathedral on the castle side was the canons' cemetery, with head- and footstones to each grave. The canons were ordained priests who were responsible for the running of the cathedral under the direction of the dean or provost. Whereas all pre-Norman and some Norman cathedrals were run by monks, who lived communally as in a monastery, the canons lived separately and met only for services, study and cathedral business. The canons' houses may have been built against the curtain wall within the cathedral precinct (see plan); others would have been further away, even outside the East Gate. The area not reserved for the canons' cemetery was a cemetery for laymen.

Bishops of Old Sarum

Herman 1048–78
(see moved from Sherborne 1075)

Osmund 1078–99
(first cathedral completed 1092)

Roger 1107–39
(greatly enlarged cathedral)

Jocelyn de Bohun 1142–84
(new west front to cathedral)

Hubert Walter 1189–94

Herbert Poore 1194–1217

Richard Poore 1217–27
(see moved to Salisbury 1219)

Early in the thirteenth century the cathedral was abandoned and a new one established in New Sarum (modern-day Salisbury). Much material was removed from Old Sarum at that time, and some of it was reused in the new cathedral where it can still be seen today, including the tombs of the first three bishops (Osmund, Roger and Jocelyn) and two round panels of stained glass. A number of elaborately carved and sculptured stones from the old cathedral are on display in Salisbury Museum. In these remains, and in the architectural splendour of the present cathedral, we can perhaps sense something of the grandeur of the great earlier cathedral built by the Normans.

The Bishop's Palace

Between the cathedral cloister and the curtain wall (about where the small fragment of wall still stands in the trees) stood the Bishop's Palace (11). As with the cathedral, only the barest foundations survive and even these have been re-covered with grass. When the transfer to Salisbury took place early in the thirteenth century all the ecclesiastical buildings were deliberately demolished, in contrast to the castle, which was simply left to decay over the centuries.

We know from the foundations that the layout of the Bishop's Palace closely resembled that of the bishop of Winchester's palace at Wolvesey, of about the same date, which is still exposed to view. The palace at Old Sarum had three ranges built around a courtyard against the curtain wall. These consisted of a Great Hall, a set of lodgings and a gatehouse. The Great Hall contained a central open hearth, a raised dais at one end, and a porch on one side. Its roof was supported by ornate columns and arches. Beside the gatehouse was a building housing the great wheel used to wind up the water bucket from a well.

The West Gate

The secondary, western entrance to Old Sarum – the West Gate (12) – can be found by walking away from the cathedral southwards, with the castle mound to your left. A rough path to the right leads to a gap in the outer bank. On either side you can see the banks and ditches built in the Iron Age and later strengthened by the Saxons and Normans. The causeway across the ditch in front is modern, replacing an earlier wooden bridge. The mound beyond, with its own outer ditch, may be an Iron Age entrance defence (or barbican), like that at the East Gate. In the Middle Ages another bridge linked this barbican with the outside world.

From the West Gate you can walk round the outer perimeter of Old Sarum back to the East Gate. This gives a good view of the spire of Salisbury Cathedral; on the skyline behind the spire a clump of trees marks Clearbury Ring, another Iron Age hillfort.

A Brief Tour of Old Sarum

1 East Gate Entrance to the Iron Age hillfort, protected by an outer mound or barbican *(page 4)*

2 Car park and toilets

3 Gatehouse A strong and imposing two-storey building guarding the entrance to the inner bailey; contained guard-chambers on the ground floor and accommodation above *(page 5)*

4 Inner bailey Inner stronghold of the Norman castle, protected by a ditch and bank and topped by a wooden wall, which was rebuilt in stone in the twelfth century *(page 6)*

5 Royal Palace Built on a grand scale by Bishop Roger for Henry I. The palace consisted of four ranges around a central courtyard and contained royal apartments and two chapels *(page 6)*

6 Keep or Great Tower The first stone building in the inner bailey, built for security. It contained royal apartments and storage space. A 'Treasure Tower' was added in the twelfth century *(page 10)*

Illustration by Terry Ball

12

6

4

13

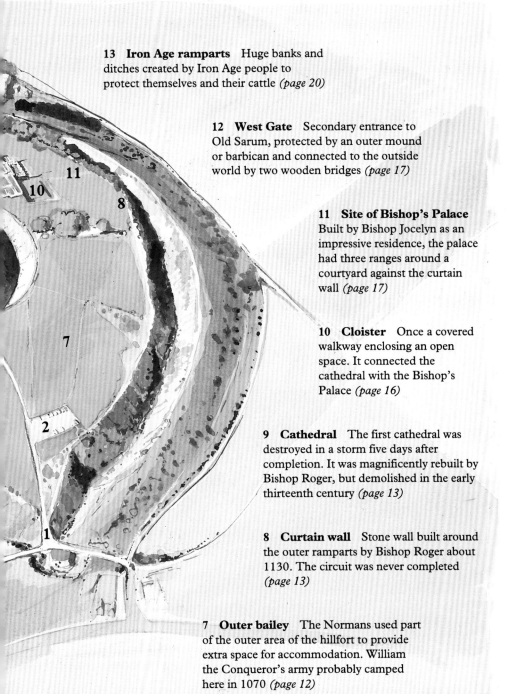

13 Iron Age ramparts Huge banks and ditches created by Iron Age people to protect themselves and their cattle *(page 20)*

12 West Gate Secondary entrance to Old Sarum, protected by an outer mound or barbican and connected to the outside world by two wooden bridges *(page 17)*

11 Site of Bishop's Palace Built by Bishop Jocelyn as an impressive residence, the palace had three ranges around a courtyard against the curtain wall *(page 17)*

10 Cloister Once a covered walkway enclosing an open space. It connected the cathedral with the Bishop's Palace *(page 16)*

9 Cathedral The first cathedral was destroyed in a storm five days after completion. It was magnificently rebuilt by Bishop Roger, but demolished in the early thirteenth century *(page 13)*

8 Curtain wall Stone wall built around the outer ramparts by Bishop Roger about 1130. The circuit was never completed *(page 13)*

7 Outer bailey The Normans used part of the outer area of the hillfort to provide extra space for accommodation. William the Conqueror's army probably camped here in 1070 *(page 12)*

A section of the Iron Age bank and ditch

The East Gate

Before you leave Old Sarum, climb the steps to the left of the toilets beside the car park. (The toilet block itself developed out of a machine-gun post put up during the Second World War.)

At the top of the steps you are standing on the bank of the Iron Age hillfort, with the site of the East Gate (now the modern entrance) immediately to your right. Attempts at a mass attack on the gate would have been blocked by the mound at the sharp bend in the lane in front of you.

The Iron Age people who built the hillfort made clever use of the terrain, cutting across the neck of a spur of Bishopsdown Hill to create a separate defensible plateau. You can appreciate from here the immense labour needed to construct the banks and ditches (13), with only crude spades and baskets as tools. In the Iron Age there would have been a wooden wall on top of the inner bank running all the way round Old Sarum – a total length of two-thirds of a mile (1km).

The Iron Age remains at Old Sarum have never been thoroughly investigated, so we can only make assumptions about how the hillfort was used. The evidence from other Iron Age sites suggests several possible interpretations. There may have been a major market at Old Sarum; alternatively, only a few people may have lived up here except in times of danger, when a whole community might have sought refuge within the protective banks. The reason for Old Sarum's great size is probably that as well as protecting people it was needed to shelter herds of cattle – the main source of wealth in the Iron Age.

When the energetic Normans took over the site 1000 years later they made all the ditches deeper and steeper-sided; the chalk rubble dug up during this operation was deposited inside the fort, thus substantially raising the level of the surface. More rubble was added this century, when excavators at the site tipped their rubble and earth here.

Looking beyond Old Sarum, you can see how the modern roads follow the straight alignment of their Roman predecessors. The road to your left leads to Marlborough, the one in front to Winchester.

When Old Sarum was at its peak, in the early Middle Ages, the area immediately outside the East Gate formed a sort of medieval suburb, accommodating the overspill from the main city. Medieval chalk quarries, lime kilns, and over seventy graves have been found to the right of the airfield in front of you (around the modern buildings).

The airfield has been in use since at least 1921. During the 1914–18 war an aircraft crashed on Old Sarum itself, demolishing a store shed that was being used by archaeologists at the time.

Walks

Here are three suggestions for one-mile (1.6km) round walks from the East Gate.

Walk 1

Turn left outside the East Gate and take the fenced footpath to the left for a complete circuit of the outer bank of the Iron Age hillfort, with views first over Salisbury Plain and then towards Salisbury Cathedral. (You can do this in the opposite direction by starting from the footpath on the right outside the gate.)

Walk 2

From the East Gate follow the entrance lane back to the main road, cross over and turn left. Look out for a large boulder in the hedge, commemorating the baseline which was accurately measured from here at the start of the Ordnance Survey of Britain in 1794. The building at the junction with Portway was the old tollhouse; it has windows in the narrow side walls so that the gate-keeper could

look out for travellers on both roads. In the eighteenth century the Portway was diverted at this point from its straight (Roman) line from Silchester to Old Sarum, so that the tollbar could not be easily bypassed. As you retrace your steps from here, you get a good view of Old Sarum.

Walk 3

Again from the East Gate, take the fenced footpath to the right of the mound at the sharp bend in the entrance lane, and turn right at the open grass field. This is the line of the Roman road to Dorchester. The hollow-way with trees almost meeting overhead is the street of the notorious 'rotten borough' of Old Sarum (see p 33). A boulder just beyond the stile on the right used to commemorate William Pitt, who sat as Member of Parliament for Old Sarum from 1734-47. The field beyond the boulder once contained the 'Parliament Tree': it was under this tree that elections – involving only two voters – took place. Either retrace your steps from here, or take the side path to the right: this leads to the West Gate or, alternatively, to Stratford sub Castle Church which contains relics of the Pitt family.

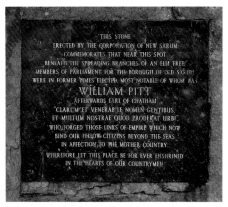

The former plaque on the Pitt memorial stone

The Story of Old Sarum

The first farmers

The earliest human visitors to the area around Old Sarum were hunters: examples of their roughly chipped stone tools have been found near Old Sarum. Their successors, between about 4000BC and 2500BC, were farmers who grew wheat and barley. Their tools included polished stone axes, usually made of local flint, although one example found at Old Sarum was of stone from Ireland and may have arrived here through the exchange of gifts. These Neolithic people built communal burial places, stock enclosures and large ritual enclosures known as henges. In certain lights it is possible to see part of a curving slope round the hilltop on which Old Sarum stands, outside the castle mound but inside the hillfort. This might mark the outline of a stock enclosure or a henge (similar to that at Avebury). Certainly, Neolithic pits have been excavated near the entrance to Old Sarum.

The Iron Age (700BC–AD43)

In the centuries before the Roman conquest the people of Salisbury Plain developed methods of intensive farming to make more efficient use of the land. The plain is covered with the low banks that mark the Iron Age field systems. These people also built hillforts, such as Old Sarum, to serve as administrative centres, cattlepounds and markets, but also as places of safety in which whole communities could shelter when under threat. Old Sarum's great outer earthwork is typically Iron Age in style and situation.

Other forts can be seen nearby, including Figsbury Ring some 3 miles (5km) to the east, and Clearbury Ring, 5 miles (8km) to the south (see map opposite). All these Iron Age hillforts seem to have been abandoned after the Roman conquest: some were actually stormed and taken by the Romans. Old Sarum is unique in this part of Wessex in having been subsequently reoccupied by the Saxons and then adapted by the Normans for their castle, cathedral and city.

The first Iron Age earthwork at Old Sarum was a simple bank with an outer ditch. The first entrance on the north side was later blocked, and an eastern entrance and a second, outer bank added. There may have been an entrance from the west as well. It is not certain whether the mounds (or barbicans) in front of the present East and West Gates date from the Iron Age, but such mounds form part of the defences of other hillforts. The hillfort may have been occupied sometime between 500BC and AD50.

A bronze belt-link of the pre-Roman period, found at Old Sarum

The Romans

We do not know if the hillfort was used to shelter the native people against the advancing Roman invaders, as happened at the hillforts at Maiden Castle and Hod Hill further west. After the conquest there was certainly some Roman settlement at Old Sarum, which is marked as SORVIODUNUM in Roman roadbooks. The only Roman walls on the site itself were found in the inner bailey during excavation of an unfinished medieval well, 17ft (5m) below the level of the castle courtyard. One possibility is that the walls belonged to a small rural shrine dedicated to a local god: such shrines are known to have been built on other hillfort sites.

A Romano-British bronze brooch dating from the first century AD and found at Old Sarum

Five important Roman roads make for Old Sarum, but they do not meet at a single point. For example, the Roman roads now called Ackling Dyke and Portway run on parallel alignments but about 500ft (150m) apart. Perhaps the whole area at the east end of Old Sarum

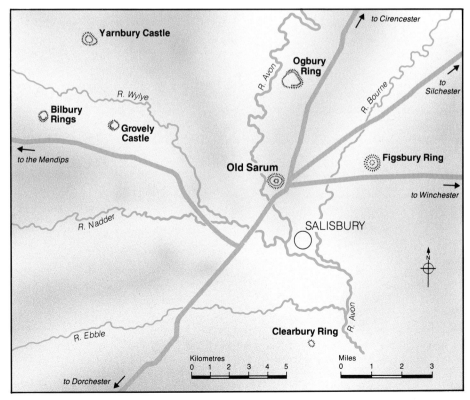

Old Sarum in relation to rivers, other Iron Age hillforts, and Roman roads

How Sarum got its name

By a lucky chance, we know what the inhabitants called Old Sarum 2000 years ago. A place is named in two Roman roadbooks at the right distance from Winchester: in one it is called SORBIODUNUM, in the other SORVIODUNUM. This must come from the earlier Celtic name SORVIADUN, 'the fortress by the gentle river' (the Avon). The Saxons mispronounced the first part of the name, and changed the second part from the Celtic 'dun' to the Germanic 'burh', both meaning 'fortress'. This resulted in the variations SEAROBYRH (in the *Anglo-Saxon Chronicle*), and SEREBRIG (the name stamped on Saxon coins).

With the arrival of the Normans the name was 'Latinised' for official purposes, sometimes being called SALISBURIA (like Salzburg, or 'city of salt', in Austria). In Domesday Book it is referred to as SARISBURIA. SARUM arose from the medieval clerks' habit of abbreviation: Sarisburia was shortened to SAR, which came to be read as Sarum. Salisbury, Sarisburia and Sarum are thus alternative names for the same place, now known as Old Sarum.

When the new town was founded in the thirteenth century all these names were transferred with it. Today of course the modern city is called Salisbury, but local people still use the name Sarum and the Bishop of Salisbury signs himself 'Sarum' on official documents.

was a Roman posting-station (like a modern motorway service area), with the roads coming in at different corners.

The Anglo-Saxons

The Romans abandoned their province of Britannia soon after AD400, leaving England open to invasion by Saxon peoples from across the North Sea. It seems likely that there was a Saxon settlement at Old Sarum, since the *Anglo-Saxon Chronicle* says that in AD552 the chieftain Cynric fought against the Britons at Searobyrg (Old Sarum) and put them to flight. Following this expulsion Old Sarum seems to have been abandoned for 300 years, but in about AD900 it was part of a large royal estate which was given to the Saxon bishopric (see) of Sherborne. The see included a huge area reaching from the south coast to the Thames Valley.

Gold ring found near Old Sarum, bearing the name of King Ethelwulf of Wessex (British Museum)

From the late ninth century onwards Alfred and later Saxon kings were under constant attack by Viking raiders. In response they organised the construction and rebuilding of fortresses for communal defence; Old Sarum's banks and ditches were strengthened at this time. The policy seems to have worked. In 1003 the market town of Wilton, about 1½ miles (2km) from Old Sarum, was sacked and burnt by the Danish king Sweyne, but Old Sarum was left alone.

Frequently, the only way the Anglo-Saxons could drive the Vikings away was by 'buying them off' with Danegeld (or tribute-money). This may have happened at Old Sarum. Before it was sacked, Wilton had had its own mint for striking coins; a year later this had been transferred to Old Sarum and three of the four Wilton moneyers were working there. A gold coin minted at Old Sarum, bearing the name of King Ethelred (978–1016), later found its way to Sweden: it is now in a museum in Stockholm.

Building operations, about 1180

communities against an invading enemy. The Normans, conversely, pioneered the use of armed cavalry operating from small forts to control the population. Instead of protecting all the people, these castles came to protect the new ruling élite. At Old Sarum this method of domination was pursued with the building of a royal castle. The adjacent town soon became a city in its own right, with its own splendid cathedral. The 150 years from the Norman Conquest to the move to New Salisbury were to be Old Sarum's greatest days.

By 1070 William the Conqueror had finally gained control over the whole country, and in March he was ready to disband his army. Old Sarum was chosen as the setting for this significant event, probably on account of its size, its position at a major crossroads and its central location in southern England. The troops were paid off with the treasure which the Anglo-Saxons had left in their minsters for safety. Those troops who had complained during the previous winter campaign in the North and Midlands were kept back for forty days as a punishment. At about the same time a document was sealed 'in the king's chamber of the castle called Salisbury': from this we can tell that the castle was already begun. By this time too the Normans were probably encouraging the growth of the old Saxon town.

A coin minted at Old Sarum which may have been paid to the Vikings as Danegeld (Royal Coin Cabinet, Stockholm)

The building of castle and cathedral

After 1066 the Normans brought many changes to English society. Wherever possible they reused old fortifications, but adapted them to serve their own rather different purposes. Hillforts such as Old Sarum had been created to protect whole

St Osmund

Osmund is said to have been William the Conqueror's nephew, and to have come over with him from Normandy in 1066. He was certainly William's chancellor (one of the chief offices in the land) from 1072 until 1078 when he was consecrated bishop of Salisbury. Osmund endowed the new cathedral with much land, but took no direct part in its management. He began to compile the system of cathedral organisation and ceremony which became known as the 'Sarum Use': later this system was widely adopted in cathedrals throughout England. In addition Osmund provided Old Sarum with a rich library, transcribing and binding some of the books himself. Sixty-five books from the old cathedral still survive, most of them in Salisbury Cathedral.

Osmund died in 1099 and subsequently miracles were claimed to have taken place at his tomb in the cathedral: one man was cured of paralysis, for example. Steps towards Osmund's canonisation began in 1228 and finally, over two centuries later and at great expense, he became St Osmund.

Manuscript from Old Sarum, thought to have belonged to Bishop Osmund (by kind permission of the Dean and Chapter of Salisbury)

As well as excelling in warfare, the Normans attached great importance to religion. A few years after the Conquest the archbishop of Canterbury, Lanfranc – a Norman appointment – ordered his bishops to transfer their headquarters from rural minsters to centres of population. This centralisation was a break with the old Anglo-Saxon traditions and was another way in which the Normans set about controlling the population.

Under the Saxons, the small rural settlement of Sherborne had been the centre of a huge diocese. In 1075 the diocesan centre was moved to Old Sarum, where, as we have seen, the castle and the beginnings of the city were already in place. The new site was also nearer the geographical centre of the diocese. At the time of the move the bishop of Sherborne was Herman, a Fleming, who had been chaplain to the Saxon king Edward the Confessor during his exile in Normandy.

A late medieval depiction of William the Conqueror with members of the Norman nobility (British Library)

Herman died in 1078, soon after the move, and it was left to his successor Osmund to build a new cathedral at Old Sarum. Both in terms of organisation and architecture, Osmund's cathedral set new standards which were soon followed in other parts of the country. Instead of being run along monastic lines, with monks living communally under the rule of an abbot, the cathedral was served by thirty-six canons living in separate lodgings under the direction of four officers: the dean, chancellor, precentor and treasurer. The architecture was Romanesque, a style associated with Normandy and other parts of Europe, and characterised by its lavish scale, designed to accommodate the elaborate processions and rituals favoured by the Normans.

In 1085 England came under the threat of invasion by Cnut of Denmark. To increase his grip on the country, William ordered an enquiry into the people and lands of England. This huge administrative survey was laboriously written up by scribes and became known as Domesday Book; part of the writing

was carried out at Old Sarum. The task was completed quickly and may have been finished by 1 August 1086: on that date all the principal landholders in England were summoned to Old Sarum to swear an oath of allegiance to William 'against all other men'. William must have recalled that the successful 1070 demobilisation had shown how convenient Old Sarum was for mass assemblies.

In 1092 Osmund's newly built cathedral was consecrated, but five days later a great storm loosened its masonry. The rebuilding and enlargement of the cathedral began soon after 1100 under the new bishop, Roger, who also built two elaborate palaces for himself and the king, in the cathedral close and the castle inner bailey respectively. (Roger was given control of the castle by Henry I in the 1130s.) But in 1139 Roger lost the favour of the new king, Stephen, who seized his

Interior of Roger's cathedral, as it might have appeared about 1130 (Peter Dunn)

Bishop Roger

Roger was a priest from Avranches in Normandy, who became the steward of Prince Henry, the youngest son of William the Conqueror. Henry was crowned king in 1100 and made Roger first his chancellor and then his justiciar. In 1102 Roger was elected bishop of Salisbury, but the archbishop of Canterbury objected to royal appointments and refused to consecrate him for five years. As bishop, Roger continued to hold enormous power in the land, even representing the king when Henry was away in Normandy. He had an exceptional knowledge of finance, supervising the collection of revenue and instituting a system of assay (checking the quality of coins). He introduced an efficient method of auditing the royal accounts using counters on a chequered cloth – hence the naming of the new government department of the 'Exchequer'.

Roger was responsible for the ambitious rebuilding of Old Sarum cathedral, begun soon after 1100. During the 1130s he also controlled the castle. Over the years Roger acquired large amounts of land and property, and by the time of Henry I's death in 1135 he held estates in Dorset and Wiltshire together with castles at Devizes, Malmesbury and Sherborne, as well as Old Sarum. The new king, Stephen, distrusted Henry's powerful chief minister and in 1139 Roger and his nephews (the bishops of Ely and Lincoln) were arrested and forced to surrender their castles. In December the same year Roger died of fever at Old Sarum, leaving gold vessels and elaborately embroidered vestments to the cathedral.

Officers receiving and weighing coin at the Exchequer, from a psalter created between 1130 and 1174 (Trinity College, Cambridge)

castles and took the money and valuables which Roger had placed on the cathedral altar for the rebuilding fund. When Roger died a few months later, the cathedral was ransacked and the new chancellor and bishop-elect, Philip de Harcourt, made off with a saint's arm covered in gold and adorned with precious stones. In 1153 King Stephen ordered the sheriff of Wiltshire to destroy the castle and part of the 'monastery' and church adjoining the castle, but the order was probably not carried out: Stephen died the next year.

After Roger, Jocelyn de Bohun was bishop of Old Sarum for more than forty years. During that time he carried out alterations to the cathedral and Bishop's Palace. Records show that Old Sarum continued to be an important administrative centre and royal base. In 1181–82 a treasury was built in the Great Tower of the castle to hold the royal treasure, and over the next few years large sums of money passed through Old Sarum, including a tax to support the Crusades. In 1189 precious royal plate was sent from Old Sarum to Westminster for the coronation of Richard I.

Bone chess piece dating from the twelfth or thirteenth century

of its authority, fame and influence: this was no time for petty squabbles to get out of hand.

After Roger's disgrace and death in 1139, the castle and city went into a decline. Henry II preferred to stay at Clarendon Palace, 4 miles (6km) south-east of Old Sarum, which was more spacious and modern than the castle and had its own hunting-park. The Sarum

The move to Salisbury

From the beginning, there was potential tension between the bishop and the military governor of the castle, who held the keys to the city gates. The problem was made worse by the intermingling of royal and ecclesiastical landholdings on the 'estate' of Old Sarum. At first the atmosphere was calmed by the mutual respect between Bishop Osmund and King William, as they pursued their complementary building projects of castle and cathedral on separate sites. The harmony continued in Bishop Roger's time, since Roger wielded both civil and ecclesiastical authority. It was during this period that Old Sarum reached the peak

Thirteenth-century bronze harness ornament

Two priests and a woman praying, from a thirteenth-century manuscript (British Library)

OLD SARUM was like Mount Gilboa: a windy, rainswept place without flowers or birds. A fortress stood on the hill, the bare chalk dazzled the eyes. The city was in the castle, and the castle, in the city. The castle was subject to the laws of Caesar, the city to those of God. The king's followers plundered the clergy.

There was a shortage of water, and a tiring climb to the top of the hill. Bishop Richard [Poore] found a better place in a well-watered valley, with a wood full of birds and animals. A new church is built beside a sparkling spring ...

Extract from a contemporary poem by Henry d'Avranches

mint was closed, and the soldiers of the castle garrison had little to do except quarrel with their neighbours at the cathedral. The clergy, for their part, complained of a building which was old-fashioned and was outshone by other cathedrals: nearby Winchester was far longer, new Canterbury more impressive. Space did not allow for the further extension which was needed to accommodate the best liturgical processions. The antagonism focused on an essential resource – water.

Although castle and cathedral had their own separate wells, the water supply seems to have been insufficient for the increasing population outside the castle. The solution to the dispute was to remove the cathedral to a new city. This idea may have been suggested by Bishop Hubert Walter who was familiar with 'planted' towns elsewhere (that is, towns that were built on a virgin site and planned out in advance).

In 1194 Bishop Herbert Poore put the idea to Richard I who approved it. By 1213 there was a detailed plan for a new

THE CANONS SAY that the cathedral church, being within the line of defence, is subject to so many inconveniences that they cannot live there without danger to life. The church needs daily repairs from wind and storm, and it is so windy that they can hardly hear one another sing and they suffer from rheumatism. There are neither trees nor grass, and the chalk is so glaring that several have gone blind. The castellan's leave is needed to go in or out, so the faithful cannot come to church if the keepers declare a danger. The clerks have to hire dwellings from the soldiers.

Mandate from the Pope to his legate, 1218

cathedral precinct down by the Avon. Four years later the crunch came, at a time of military tension in southern England. The dean and clergy of Old Sarum, returning from a procession to St Martin's church at Milford, outside the city gates, found the East Gate barred. The garrison said they had feared a foreign attack – probably a trumped-up excuse. This humiliation of the clergy was the last straw. Pope Honorius III was petitioned and gave his agreement to the removal of the cathedral to a new site. The townsfolk had already been moving away from the hill to the valley, so the bishop was following rather than leading his flock. The quarrelling neighbours were parted, the clergy and townsfolk had room to expand, and both merchant and landowner (in this case the bishop) found a fresh source of revenue in a new centre for trade. In this they were imitating the bishop of Winchester, who had recently founded several new towns on trade routes in his diocese, although he did not need to move his cathedral.

New Sarum

In 1219 a wooden chapel was put up in the Myrfield, a meadow beside a curve of the River Avon, and a market licence was obtained by Bishop Richard Poore. The new cathedral was founded in 1220 and was largely completed by 1250, although the famous spire was not added until the beginning of the fourteenth century. As at Old Sarum, the cathedral was surrounded by the canons' houses and Bishop's Palace, ringing the cemetery area.

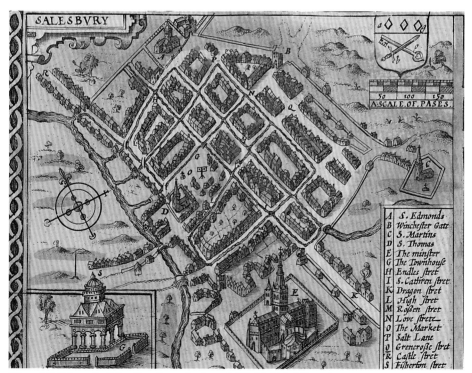

Plan of Salisbury by John Speed, made about 1600 (British Library)

The town covered 260 acres (105ha), nearly ten times the size of Old Sarum, one-third being the new cathedral precinct. It was planned as a grid, with water from the river being diverted to serve each 'chequer' (or square of the grid) – no lack of water here! A yearly fair began in 1221 and four years later the town was granted its charter as a free city, modelled on Winchester. The principal trade was in wool fleeces and, later on, in finished woollen cloth.

From city to rotten borough

The old cathedral was effectively abandoned in 1226 when the tombs of its three principal bishops – Osmund, Roger and Jocelyn – were removed to the new cathedral. One chapel was kept up within the old cathedral precinct. The Bishop's Palace went to the Crown, but in 1236 it was demolished and the timber and stone were carted into the castle. A century later the remaining stones of the old cathedral and the canons' houses were taken away to form the wall of the new cathedral close.

The burgesses of Old Sarum complained about the new market, which was taking away their business, but Old Sarum remained a useful trading

crossroads until 1244, when a new bridge allowed Salisbury traffic to bypass both Wilton and Old Sarum. In 1377 there were only ten poll-tax payers in Old Sarum, compared with 3,226 in New Salisbury (this was a head-tax, from which we can tell the number of inhabitants). Old Sarum still had a mayor in 1422, but much of the old town was already overgrown and buried. By 1540 there was not one house left standing. Most of the building materials had been taken away for use in Salisbury.

The castle was kept up as the official residence of the sheriff of Wiltshire. The system of regular castleguard (soldiers to guard the castle) lapsed in 1255, but the castle was recommissioned during the Barons' War against Henry III a few years later. The gaol was in use until 1447 when the castle was granted to Sir John Stourton, although a mass break-out by prisoners in 1336 suggests that it was not always in good condition. In 1514 Henry VIII allowed Thomas Compton, groom to his chamber, to carry away the stone from the castle, marking its final demise.

Despite this dilapidation and depopulation, Old Sarum sent members to Parliament for over 500 years, from 1295 to 1832 (with a break in the

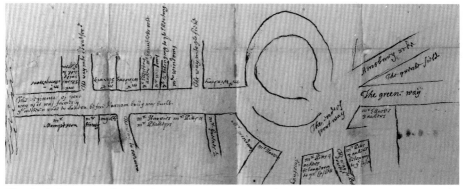

Sketch of about 1700 showing the Old Sarum 'burgage plots'. The 'electing acre' was made up of the narrowest strips at the top left of the picture (Salisbury and South Wilts Museum)

Caricature showing those for and against the 1832 Reform Bill. 'Old Sarum' appears on one of the lower left-hand branches (British Museum)

fourteenth century). By the late seventeenth century Old Sarum had become both a 'pocket borough' – meaning it was owned by a private individual – and a 'rotten borough' – meaning that it had no real voters. The owner controlled election results and could therefore be certain that his candidate – usually himself – would be returned to Parliament.

The way elections worked was that the owner granted short leases on two plots of land (burgage plots) adjoining 'The Parliament Tree', an elm which stood in the old marketplace. The leaseholders voted, in a tent pitched under the elm, for the owner's nominee. They then gave up their leases. Thomas Pitt, who had made his fortune in the East Indies, bought the castle site and sat as MP for Old Sarum in 1689–90 and then from 1705–26. William

Pitt, later earl of Chatham, was MP from 1734–47. In 1804 the seat was bought by Lord Caledon.

By the Great Reform Act of 1832 Old Sarum's seat in Parliament was abolished. During the campaign leading up to the passing of the act, Old Sarum had been cited as one of the most notorious examples of the unfair and outdated electoral system. Branches were later taken from the Parliament Tree and made into souvenirs. The trunk of the elm survived until 1905. Old Sarum was placed in the care of the nation in 1892. It is now looked after by English Heritage.

Buried Sarum is unearthed

In Tudor times the site of Old Sarum reverted to pasture land and so it has remained ever since. In 1834, however,

The excavation team in July 1914.
Lieutenant Colonel Hawley is on the left
(Salisbury and South Wilts Museum)

very dry weather showed up the plan of
the cathedral in the parched grass; it was
subsequently measured and partly
excavated. Twenty years later, a skeleton
with a chalice and a funerary paten (a
shallow circular plate) was dug up outside
the entrance to Old Sarum; perhaps these
were the remains of one of the cathedral
canons.

The Society of Antiquaries of London
instigated excavations on the site of the
castle between 1909 and 1911 and that of
the cathedral in 1912–15. The historical
and architectural reports were written by
Sir William St John Hope, although he

Looking to the outer bailey and beyond from
the castle gatehouse, 1909. The railway track
was constructed to carry away the spoil from
the excavations (Salisbury and South Wilts
Museum)

only visited the site intermittently. The
daily digging was controlled by Lieutenant
Colonel William Hawley, and was run like
a military operation.

Practically no masonry was visible
before the excavations started. Between 8
and 10ft (2.5 and 3m) of soil had to be
dug away from the sites of the castle and
the cathedral to expose the walls that you
see today. A light railway track was laid,
complete with points, so that hand-
pushed trucks could carry away the spoil,
much of which was then spread over the
outer bailey. The loose flints were sold off
(for road or building material) to help
finance the excavations, to which John
Pierpont Morgan, an American financier,
was a generous contributor.

Following excavation, the Society of
Antiquaries and the government Office of
Works consolidated the medieval walls by
covering them with turf strips or by
bringing them up to a smooth face with
flints and cement mortar (as at the Great
Tower, for instance). They inserted dated
stones to mark their work, which now in
turn is in need of repair – this will be
undertaken by English Heritage. Most of
the finds from the early twentieth-century
excavations can be seen in Salisbury and
South Wiltshire Museum.

Excavations did not continue after the
First World War, owing to the depth of
the soil that would have had to be cleared,
and uncertainty about what might remain
to be discovered. The Society of
Antiquaries instead turned its attention to
Stonehenge in the 1920s and to
Clarendon Palace in the '30s.

The future of Old Sarum

In recent years, conservation work at Old
Sarum has focused on the ecology as
much as the archaeology. The site lies on
chalk downland with a gravel capping and
a thin soil layer under the turf. An

Old Sarum *by John Constable, 1834 (Victoria and Albert Museum)*

attractive beech plantation 'hangs' on the outer banks overlooking Salisbury, and here and there are some earlier yew trees. The area is host to a variety of natural habitats and boasts many species of plants and birds. The Wiltshire Trust for Nature Conservation has identified 20 different species of tree, as many grasses and over 100 different wild flowers. The beech 'hanger' provides a habitat for birds, especially warblers.

This varied ecology, overlying vulnerable archaeological remains, requires careful management. Up to about 1950 the site was grazed by sheep and rabbits, but when grazing ceased new trees and shrubs seeded themselves and threatened to take over. As well as damaging the archaeological remains this reduced the variety of natural habitats, as particular species came to dominate. In response to these problems, much of the scrub has been cleared. In future, regular cutting and coppicing will maintain a proper balance between plant species.

The relationship between man and nature has been a constant theme throughout Old Sarum's long history. As early as 4000BC Neolithic people began the process of opening up the forest and turning it into farmland. By the Iron Age the population had grown to such an extent that territorial conflicts developed between rival communities; at this time the hillfort was built for communal defence. Until the early Middle Ages the story is one of man's gradual encroachment on the landscape, reaching a peak with the completion of the Norman castle and city, and Bishop Roger's great cathedral. From the time of the move to New Salisbury this process went into reverse, as the buildings collapsed, the stone was carried away, and nature began to take over. Now, through sensitive conservation, it is hoped that Old Sarum's unique character will be preserved and that visitors will continue to enjoy the site both for its rich history and its natural beauty.

Further Reading

Discovery and excavation

The Gentleman's Magazine, 1795, I,
193–4; 1796, I, 185–6; 1834, II, 418;
1835, II, 143–6, 540, 640

R Benson and H Hatcher, 1843. *The
history of Old and New Sarum or Salisbury*
(vol VI of R Colt Hoare, *History of Modern
Wiltshire*)

Archaeologia, 1855, XXXVI, 183

*Proceedings of the Society of Antiquaries of
London*, 1910–11, xxiii, 190–201, 501–18;
1912, xxiv, 52–65; 1913, xxv, 93–104;
1914, xxvi, 100–19; 1915, xxvii, 230–40;
1916, xxviii, 174–83

Antiquaries' Journal, 1935, XV, 174–92;
1936, XVI; 1948, XXVI

Archaeological Journal, 1947, CIV, 128–39

Wiltshire Archaeological Magazine, 1945,
51, 259–69; 1956, 56, 102–26; 1960, 57,
171–91, 352–70; 1962, 59, 130–54

General history

H de S Shortt (ed), 1957. *The City of
Salisbury*

G N Garmonsway (ed), 1960. *The
Anglo-Saxon Chronicle*

Victoria County History of Wiltshire,
1955–62, vols 2, 3, 5, and especially 6,
53–60

J Chandler, 1983. *Endless Street: a history
of Salisbury and its people*

Historical fiction

E Rutherfurd, 1987. *Sarum: the Novel of
England*

Architectural history

J P Bushe-Fox, 1937. *Old Sarum, Wiltshire*

H M Colvin (ed), 1963. *History of the
King's Works*, II, 824–8

H de S Shortt, 1965. *Old Sarum, Wiltshire*

*Journal of the British Archaeological
Association*, 1971, third series, XXXIV,
62–83

Royal Commission on Historical
Monuments, 1980. *The City of Salisbury* I
(excluding cathedral and close, for which
now see the 1993–7 monographs on each)

T B James and A M Robinson, 1988.
Clarendon Palace (Research Report 45 of
the Society of Antiquaries of London, and
also a summary booklet available from
Salisbury Museum)

R D H Gem, 1990. 'The first
Romanesque Cathedral at Old Salisbury',
in *Medieval Architecture and its Intellectual
Context: studies in honour of Peter Kidson*
(ed E Fernie and P Crossley)

Ecclesiastical history

W H Jones, 1879. *Fasti Ecclesiae
Sarisberiensis* and 1883/4. *The Register of
St Osmund*

A R Malden, 1901. *The canonisation of
St Osmund*, Wiltshire Records Society